JONAH AND THE BIG FISH

Bible Bedtime Story

BLUME POTTER

INTRODUCTION

In a world filled with countless stories, there are few as timeless and powerful as those found in the Bible. Jonah and the Big Fish is one such story—an adventure that not only captivates the imagination but also imparts valuable life lessons that your children or grandchildren will carry with them for years to come.

This beautifully crafted book brings the story of Jonah to life in a way that is both engaging and accessible for young minds. Each chapter is filled with excitement, from the mighty storm that shakes the ship to Jonah's miraculous journey inside the belly of a big fish. But beyond the thrilling narrative, this story teaches essential lessons about obedience, forgiveness, and the boundless love and mercy of God.

As you settle down to read this Bible bedtime story with your little ones, you'll find that it opens up opportunities for meaningful conversations about faith and the importance of making the right choices, even when it's difficult. This book is more than just a bedtime story; it's a tool to instill values that will help shape the character of the next generation.

We invite you to share in Jonah's adventure, to experience the wonder of God's love, and to pass on these timeless lessons to your children or grandchildren. With each reading, you're not just telling a story—you're helping to build a foundation of faith that will last a lifetime.

CHAPTER 1:
JONAH RUNS AWAY

In the bustling town of Gath-hepher, where the sun shone brightly and the birds sang sweetly, lived a man named Jonah. Jonah was a prophet, someone who listened to God and shared His messages with the people. One day, as Jonah was tending to his small garden, he heard a voice—a voice he knew well. It was God, speaking to him in the soft whispers of the wind.

"Jonah," the voice called gently, "I have an important task for you. The people of Nineveh are doing many bad things, and I need you to go there and tell them to change their ways."

Jonah's heart skipped a beat. Nineveh! The very name made him frown. He had heard all about the people of Nineveh—how they were cruel and did terrible things. Why would God want to help them? Jonah thought to himself. They didn't deserve it! He didn't want to go to Nineveh, not one bit.

So, Jonah made a decision. He would run away, far away from Nineveh and from God's command. He packed a small bag, taking only what he needed, and set off toward the sea. When he reached the bustling port, filled with the smell of saltwater and the sound of seagulls cawing, he found a ship that was heading to a faraway place called Tarshish, in the exact opposite direction of Nineveh.

"One ticket to Tarshish, please," Jonah said to the ship's captain, his voice trembling just a little.

The captain, a gruff man with a big bushy beard, took the coins Jonah handed him and nodded. "Board quickly; we set sail soon," he said.

Jonah hurried onto the ship, his heart pounding. As the ship's crew prepared to leave, Jonah found a quiet corner below deck, away from the other passengers. He sat down, pulling his bag close, and tried to calm his racing thoughts. "Surely," Jonah thought, "if I go far enough, God will find someone else to send to Nineveh. I'll be safe in Tarshish, away from that dreadful place."

The ship set sail, the wooden hull creaking as it moved through the waves. Jonah felt a strange mix of relief and worry. He was running away, but deep down, he knew that running away from what God wanted was never a good idea. Still, he closed his eyes, hoping that maybe, just maybe, he could forget all about Nineveh and the people he didn't want to help.

As the ship sailed farther from shore, Jonah began to feel the gentle rocking of the waves, and soon, he drifted off to sleep, thinking he had left all his troubles behind.

But Jonah was in for a surprise. Running away from God's plans was not as easy as he thought. Little did Jonah know, his adventure was just beginning, and the sea held more than just water—it held a lesson that Jonah would never forget.

CHAPTER 2:
A MIGHTY STORM

As Jonah slept soundly below deck, the ship sailed further into the vast, open sea. But soon, the calm waters began to change. Dark clouds gathered overhead, and the gentle breeze turned into a fierce wind. The waves grew taller and stronger, crashing against the ship with a force that made the wooden planks creak and groan.

The sailors, seasoned men who had faced many storms before, quickly realized this was no ordinary storm. The wind howled like a wild beast, and the sea tossed the ship back and forth as if it were a toy. The sailors' faces turned pale with fear.

"Throw the cargo overboard!" shouted the captain, trying to steady the ship. "We need to lighten the load!"

The sailors hurried to obey, tossing crates of goods into the raging sea. But no matter how much they threw overboard, the storm only grew worse. The ship was being tossed about like a leaf in the wind, and the sailors began to panic. They cried out to their gods, pleading for the storm to stop, but nothing worked.

Meanwhile, below deck, Jonah was jolted awake by the violent rocking of the ship. He stumbled to his feet, his heart pounding as he realized what was happening. This storm—it wasn't just any storm. It was sent by God, and Jonah knew exactly why.

He hurried up to the deck, where the sailors were desperately trying to keep the ship from capsizing. "It's my fault!" Jonah shouted over the roar of the wind and waves. "This storm is because of me! I'm running away from God's command."

The sailors looked at him in shock and disbelief. "What should we do?" one of them asked, his voice trembling.

"Throw me into the sea," Jonah said, his voice steady despite the chaos around him. "If you do, the storm will stop."

The sailors hesitated. They didn't want to throw an innocent man overboard, but they also knew they were running out of options. With the ship on the brink of sinking, they decided to do as Jonah said.

They lifted Jonah and, with heavy hearts, threw him into the churning sea. The moment Jonah hit the water, the storm began to calm. The wind died down, the waves grew smaller, and soon, the sea was as peaceful as it had been before.

The sailors were amazed and filled with awe. They knew then that Jonah's God was powerful, and they prayed to Him, thanking Him for sparing their lives. But as the sea grew calm, Jonah began to sink deeper into the water, knowing that his adventure was far from over.

CHAPTER 3:
IN THE BELLY OF THE FISH

The moment Jonah hit the water, the storm ceased, and the sea became as calm as a glassy pond. But before Jonah could take a breath, the water around him began to churn again—this time, not from a storm, but from something much bigger. A huge fish, sent by God, appeared from the depths and swallowed Jonah whole.

Inside the belly of the fish, it was dark and damp. The smell of the sea was strong, and the only sound was the soft gurgle of the fish's movements. Jonah sat there, feeling the weight of his choices pressing down on him. He was alive, but he was trapped, deep beneath the waves, with nothing to do but think.

For three days and three nights, Jonah remained in the belly of the fish. During that time, he reflected on what had brought him here—his fear, his stubbornness, and his attempt to run away from God. He realized that no matter how far he tried to go, he couldn't escape God's presence or His plan.

Jonah's heart grew heavy with regret. He knew he had made a mistake, and he also knew that only God could save him now. So, in the quiet darkness, Jonah prayed. He prayed with all his heart, asking God for forgiveness. He admitted that he had been wrong to run away and promised that if given another chance, he would obey God's command, no matter where it led him.

As Jonah prayed, he felt a sense of peace washing over him. He knew that God had heard him and that he was not alone, even in the belly of a fish. Jonah's prayer was sincere, and he was ready to follow God's will, trusting that it was the right path.

The fish continued to swim through the vast ocean, and Jonah waited, knowing that his fate was in God's hands. He didn't know what would happen next, but he was no longer afraid. He had learned an important lesson about obedience and faith, and he was ready to face whatever came next.

CHAPTER 4:
JONAH'S SECOND CHANCE

After three days and nights in the belly of the big fish, Jonah's heartfelt prayers reached God's ears. God, in His great mercy, decided to give Jonah a second chance. He commanded the fish to spit Jonah out onto dry land.

With a mighty heave, the fish swam towards the shore and opened its mouth wide. In a moment, Jonah found himself back on solid ground, covered in seaweed but very much alive. He took a deep breath of fresh air, feeling the warmth of the sun on his face. Jonah knew that this was his second chance—a chance he would not waste.

This time, Jonah didn't hesitate. He shook off the sand and seaweed, and without a second thought, he set off for Nineveh. The journey was long, but Jonah's heart was determined. He knew what he had to do.

When Jonah finally arrived in Nineveh, the city was bustling with people. The buildings were tall, and the streets were crowded, but Jonah was not intimidated. He walked through the city, calling out to the people, "Listen to me! God has sent me to warn you. You must stop doing bad things, or your city will be destroyed!"

To Jonah's surprise, the people of Nineveh stopped and listened. They saw the sincerity in Jonah's eyes and heard the truth in his words. The news spread quickly, and soon the whole city was talking about Jonah's message. The people of Nineveh, from the poorest to the richest, decided to change their ways. They stopped doing bad things and began to live in a way that pleased God.

Jonah watched in amazement as the city transformed. He had expected the people to ignore him, but instead, they had listened and taken his words to heart. Jonah realized that God's plans were always for the best, even if he didn't understand them at first.

With Nineveh turning away from its wicked ways, Jonah knew that he had fulfilled his mission. He had learned that God is merciful and that everyone deserves a second chance—even the people of Nineveh, and even himself.

CHAPTER 5:
GOD'S LOVE AND MERCY

Jonah sat on a hill overlooking Nineveh, watching as the people turned from their bad ways and began to live better lives. But instead of feeling joy, Jonah felt a deep sense of frustration. He had hoped that God would punish the people of Nineveh for their wrongdoings, but instead, God had shown them mercy.

"Why, God?" Jonah muttered to himself. "Why did you forgive them? They deserved to be punished for all the bad things they've done."

As Jonah sat sulking, God spoke to him, asking, "Jonah, do you have a right to be angry?"

Jonah didn't answer right away. He was still upset, but he knew that God's question was important. God continued, "Jonah, you were concerned about a plant that grew up overnight and then withered away. Should I not be concerned about Nineveh, a city filled with thousands of people who didn't know right from wrong? I care about them, just as I care about you."

Jonah thought about God's words. He realized that he had been too focused on his own feelings and not enough on God's love and mercy. God cared about everyone, even those who made mistakes. Jonah had learned that it wasn't his place to decide who deserved forgiveness. That was God's job, and God's love was far greater than Jonah had imagined.

As Jonah sat on the hill, he finally understood the lesson God was teaching him. It wasn't about punishment; it was about mercy and the chance to change. God had given the people of Nineveh a second chance, just as He had given Jonah a second chance when he was in the belly of the fish.

Jonah bowed his head and prayed, "Thank you, God, for showing me your love and mercy. I understand now that your ways are always right, even when I don't see it at first. Help me to follow your instructions, no matter how difficult they may seem."

With that prayer, Jonah's heart was at peace. He had learned that God's love was for everyone, and that mercy was a gift that could change lives. Jonah knew that he would carry this lesson with him for the rest of his days.

Printed in the USA
CPSIA information can be obtained
at www.ICGtesting.com
CBHW080850111024
15667CB00046B/805

9 798330 438983